EFFECTIVE
MEETING

KT-383-591

to be returned on or before
st date stamped below

Better Management Skills

This highly popular range of inexpensive paperbacks covers all areas of basic management. Practical, easy to read and instantly accessible, these guides will help managers to improve their business or communication skills. Those marked * are available on audio cassette.

The books in this series can be tailored to specific company requirements. For further details, please contact the publisher, Kogan Page, telephone 0171-278 0433, fax 0171-837 6348.

Be a Successful Supervisor
Business Etiquette
Business Creativity
Coaching Your Employees
Conducting Effective Interviews
Counselling Your Staff
Creative Decision-making
Creative Thinking in Business
Effective Employee Participation
Effective Meeting Skills
Effective Performance Appraisals*
Effective Presentation Skills
Empowerment
First Time Supervisor
Get Organised!
Goals and Goal Setting
How to Communicate Effectively*
How to Develop a Positive Attitude*
How to Develop Assertiveness
How to Motivate People*
How to Understand Financial
    Statements
How to Write a Staff Manual
Improving Employee Performance
Improving Relations at Work
Keeping Customers for Life
Leadership Skills for Women
Learning to Lead
Make Every Minute Count*

Making TQM Work
Managing Cultural Diversity at
    Work
Managing Disagreement
    Constructively
Managing Organisational Change
Managing Part-Time Employees
Managing Quality Customer Service
Managing Your Boss
Marketing for Success
Memory Skills in Business
Mentoring
Office Management
Personnel Testing
Productive Planning
Project Management
Quality Customer Service
Rate Your Skills as a Manager
Sales Training Basics
Self-managing Teams
Selling Professionally
Successful Negotiation
Successful Presentation Skills
Successful Telephone Techniques
Systematic Problem-solving and
    Decision-making
Team Building
Training Methods that Work
The Woman Manager

EFFECTIVE MEETING · SKILLS ·

Marion E Haynes

**KOGAN
PAGE**

First published in the United States of America in 1988
by Crisp Publications Inc, 1200 Hamilton Court,
Menlo Park, Los Altos, California 94025, USA

This edition first published in Great Britain in 1988
by Kogan Page Ltd, 120 Pentonville Road, London N1 9JN

Reprinted 1989 (twice), 1991, 1994, 1996

British Library Cataloguing in Publication Data

Haynes, Marion E.
  Effective meeting skills.
  1. Meetings. Organisation – Manuals
  I. Title
  658.4′563

  ISBN 1–85091–759–0 Pbk

Typeset by DP Photosetting, Aylesbury, Bucks
Printed and bound in Great Britain by
Biddles Ltd, Guildford

Contents

Preface

Meetings are commonplace in modern civilisation. In addition to the meetings that take place during working hours, nearly everyone at one time or another is a member of a professional society, civic association, parents' association, or religious group. With meetings occurring so frequently one could expect them to be a source of satisfaction and accomplishment. However, this is often not the case.

Effective Meeting Skills was designed to help you improve the quality of meetings you attend either as the leader, or as a participant. It begins with the premise that an effective meeting is one that achieves its objectives within a reasonable time. The book is divided into five chapters which tell you how to participate in more effective meetings. They are:

1. Introduction
2. Planning Meetings
3. Conducting Meetings
4. Improving Meetings
5. Summary and Conclusion

Throughout the book are questionnaires, checklists, and exercises that emphasise the material presented. Work through these as you go along. They serve as an excellent means of verifying your understanding.

Effective meetings are within your grasp. Simply read, understand, and apply the ideas contained in this book.

CHAPTER 1
Introduction

Objectives for the reader

Objectives give a sense of purpose and direction. They define what is to be accomplished and help to provide a sense of fulfilment when they are achieved. From the list below, tick the objectives that are important to you.

By completing this book I plan to:

- ☐ Learn how to accomplish more in the meetings I hold or attend.
- ☐ Learn how to make decisions in meetings that are of high quality and supported by everyone.
- ☐ Learn how to conduct meetings where everyone participates.
- ☐ Learn how to spend less time in meetings.

What is a meeting and what makes one effective?

What is a meeting?
A meeting can be defined as a gathering of three or more people sharing common objectives, where communication (verbal and/or written) is the primary means of achieving those objectives.

When is a meeting effective?
A meeting is effective when it achieves its objectives in minimum time to the satisfaction of the participants.

This book will teach you how to conduct effective meetings

and how to contribute to their success as a participant. The content is directed towards these three criteria:

1. Achieve the objectives of the meeting
2. Use a minimum amount of time
3. Satisfy the participants

Evaluate a meeting

Consider the typical meeting you attend whether in business, at church, in a club, etc. Compare your meetings with the following characteristics of an effective meeting. Tick those statements that apply to meetings you normally conduct or attend:

☐ 1. An agenda is prepared priop to the meeting.
☐ 2. Meeting participants have an opportunity to contribute to the agenda.
☐ 3. Advance notice of meeting time and place is provided to those invited.
☐ 4. Meeting facilities are comfortable and adequate for the number of participants.
☐ 5. The meeting begins on time.
☐ 6. The meeting has a scheduled ending time.
☐ 7. The use of time is monitored throughout the meeting.
☐ 8. Everyone has an opportunity to present his or her point of view.
☐ 9. Participants listen attentively to one another.
☐ 10. There are periodic summaries as the meeting progresses.
☐ 11. No one tends to dominate the discussion.
☐ 12. Everyone has a voice in decisions made at the meeting.
☐ 13. The meeting usually ends with a summary of accomplishments.
☐ 14. The meeting is periodically evaluated by participants.
☐ 15. People can be depended on to carry out any action agreed during the meeting.
☐ 16. A memorandum of discussion or minutes of the meeting is provided to each participant following the meeting.
☐ 17. The meeting leader follows up with participants on action agreed during the meeting.

☐ 18. The appropriate and necessary people can be counted on to attend each meeting.

☐ 19. The decision process used is appropriate for the size of the group.

☐ 20. When used, audio-visual equipment is in good working condition and does not detract from the meeting.

Number of statements ticked _____ × 5 = _____ Meeting score

A score of 80 or more indicates you attend a high percentage of quality meetings. A score below 60 suggests work is required to improve the quality of meetings you attend.

Types of meetings

Meetings can be classified into two major categories. Each category has two subsets:

Information meetings
- Advise/update
- Sell

and

Decision-making meetings
- Goal setting
- Problem solving

This classification is helpful because each type of meeting must be conducted differently. By studying the chart on the next page, you will learn the differences between the two types. Use this chart to classify your meetings and then decide the proper way to plan for each type.

Key differences in types of meetings

Elements	Information meeting	Decision-making meeting
Number of attenders	Any number	Preferably not more than 12
Who should attend	Those who need to know	Those responsible and those who can contribute
Communication process	One way from leader to participants with opportunities for questions	Interactive discussion among all attending
Meeting room set-up	Participants facing front of room – classroom style	Participants facing each other – conference style
Most effective style of leadership	Authoritative	Participative
Emphasis should be on	Content	Interaction and problem-solving
Key to success	Planning and preparation of information to be presented	Meeting climate that supports open, free expression

Problems with meetings

Write down three things about meetings you attend that bother you.

1. _____

2. _____

3. _____

Many people who regularly participate in meetings report a majority to be ineffective. For example, one survey* of 635 executives showed that 75 per cent of them were bothered by the ineffectiveness of typical meetings they attend. Their reasons are summarised below. Compare your reaction to the meetings you attend with the following negative meeting characteristics.

Meeting characteristic	Bothered a lot %
Drifting off subject	83
Poor preparation	77
Questionable effectiveness	74
Lack of listening	68
Verbosity of participants	62
Length	60
Lack of participation	51

From this list it is clear what needs to be done.

Solutions to common meeting problems
Tick those you plan to implement or improve:

☐ *State your objective*
Every meeting needs objectives. They should be clearly presented in the leader's opening statement. This simple procedure establishes the reason for the meeting. With an objective in mind, all discussion and energy can be directed towards it.

---

* 'Achieving Effective Meetings – Not Easy But Possible' by Bradford D Smart, *Training and Development Journal*, 1974. American Society for Training and Development reprinted with permission. All rights reserved.

☐ *Prepare an agenda*
An agenda is essential. It should be prepared in advance and given to participants *before* the meeting. It will serve as a road map to keep discussion on the topic. When distributed before a meeting an agenda encourages advance preparation.

☐ *Be selective when picking participants*
You want the minimum number of appropriate people. Smaller numbers will hold interest and increase participation. You may need to contact some people before the meeting to explain your reason for not including them.

☐ *Manage meeting time*
Strike a balance between wasting time and rushing the group. Allow sufficient time for participants to become involved and feel satisfied with the outcome. Start on time, keep things moving towards an announced ending time.

☐ *Take charge*
Effective control and guidance are required for effective meetings. Use the agenda to keep the discussion on topic. Encourage less active participants. Control those who attempt to dominate. Decide in advance the best procedures for achieving the meeting's objective and use them at appropriate times.

☐ *Close with a summary*
Every meeting should close with a restatement of the meeting's objective, a summary of what was accomplished towards the objective, and a review of agreed action that needs to be taken.

Check what you learned in Chapter 1

Consider the following statements and mark each one true or false based on the material in Chapter 1.

True/False

_____ 1. A meeting relies on communication to achieve its objective.

_____ 2. A gathering must have at least three participants to qualify as a meeting.

_____ 3. An effective meeting must consider the satisfaction of all participants.

_____ 4. Effective meetings can consume unlimited time.

_____ 5. Information meetings are best conducted in a participative style.

_____ 6. Decision-making meetings can be conducted through interactive group discussions.

_____ 7. Decision-making meetings can be conducted with any number of participants.

_____ 8. A majority of business executives are bothered by the ineffectiveness of the meetings they attend.

_____ 9. Drifting off the subject is a common complaint about meetings.

_____ 10. There is nothing a leader can do to control inappropriate discussion during a meeting.

See page 94 for recommended responses.

CHAPTER 2
Planning Meetings

To meet or not to meet

The first consideration when planning a meeting is whether or not one is required. All too often, holding a meeting is a foregone conclusion when it should be a carefully considered decision.

Whether or not to hold a meeting should start with a statement of objectives. What is the end result you expect to achieve through a meeting? Is a meeting the best way to achieve this objective?

Examples of a meeting objectives

- To inform our department of changes in the holiday pay policy.
- To persuade management to adopt our division's plan to computerise the payroll.
- To decide the best way to solve the Chamber of Commerce budget deficit.
- To decide realistic sales goals for each district, based on the company's overall sales goals for next year.
- To decide the critical skills required for successful performance as a first level supervisor.

With objectives clearly stated, you can then decide the best way to achieve them. It may turn out that a meeting is appropriate. Or it may turn out that a memorandum, bulletin board posting, or series of phone calls, would be a better means of disseminating information.

Checklists to decide whether a meeting is required

Information meetings

Consideration	Yes	No
• Is time of the essence?	____	____
• Is the group geographically dispersed?	____	____
• Does the size of the group make a meeting feasible, say 10 to 100?	____	____
• Is it imperative that everyone fully understands the information?	____	____
• Is the information being presented needed later as reference material?	____	____

Decision-making meetings

Consideration	Yes	No
• Is the knowledge required for any problem-solving dispersed among several people?	____	____
• Is the commitment of several people required for successful implementation of the results?	____	____
• Can the synergy of group interaction contribute to a quality decision?	____	____
• Are there likely to be conflicting points of view which need to be reconciled?	____	____
• Are there questions of fairness that need to be resolved?	____	____

Developing an agenda

Every meeting should have an agenda and it should be given (in advance, if possible) to each participant. Ideally, participants should have an opportunity to contribute to an agenda prior to the meeting.

An agenda need not be an elaborate document. It can be handwritten and photocopied. It can be written on a chalkboard or flipchart. If there are only two or three items on it, it can be communicated orally.

Be guided in the preparation of any published agenda by the needs of participants. What do they need to know to participate effectively in the meeting? The following elements should be included:

- Date, place and time
- Items to be dealt with (listed in proper sequence)
- Meeting adjournment time
- Time of scheduled breaks, if any

As leader of a meeting, you need more detail than the participants. For example, you should have a rough time allocation for each item to gauge the progress of the meeting properly. Also, you may need notes on techniques to use, points to be clarified, and equipment that may be required.

When sending an agenda prior to a meeting, think about who should receive a copy. Decide who should have a copy strictly for information and who you expect to attend and participate in the meeting. Address your communication to those you expect to attend. Show the 'information only' recipients as cc's. This will clear up any uncertainty over who is expected to attend.

Regularly scheduled staff or committee meetings seem to be the most common violators of the agenda requirement. One way to overcome this problem is to take five minutes at the beginning of the meeting to develop and announce an agenda. If there are several items on your agenda, put them in order of priority so you can deal with the most important ones in the time available. Also, if new items come up during the meeting, they can be added to the agenda in proper priority order.

Specimen agenda

- Opening statement – reason for attendance, objective, time commitment
- Problems to be discussed
- Generate alternative solutions
- Decide among alternatives
- Develop plan to solve problem
- Assign tasks to carry out plan
- Establish follow-up procedures
- Summarise and adjourn

Prepare an agenda for your next meeting

Think of a meeting you are likely to conduct in the near future. Consider items to be discussed and the sequence in which they should be handled. Estimate the time required for each item. From this estimate, set a tentative ending time. (*Note.* This should be considered a tentative agenda until it is discussed with and confirmed by participants.)

Agenda item	Time estimate

Selecting participants

When selecting meeting participants, the best guideline is to have the smallest number of appropriate people. This isn't always easy. There will often be people who feel they should come but are unable to contribute or gain from attendance. Also, there may be people you feel should be invited because of their position in the organisation, but they too may have nothing to contribute.

The only feasible method for selecting participants is to consider the type of meeting you are planning. If it is to be an information meeting, you want attenders who need to know the information being presented. If it is a problem-solving meeting, you need participants who have knowledge to contribute, authority over the area affected by the decision, and the commitment to carry out the decision.

Prior to the meeting, give some thought to those who might wish to attend but do not appear on your participant list. To maintain good relationships, it may be wise to explain the objective of your meeting and why you feel they do not have to attend. They will probably react by:

- Agreeing with you and thanking you for your thoughtfulness
- Disagreeing with you and presenting reasons which may cause you to change your mind
- Disagreeing with you, but requiring you to stand firm on their exclusion.

On the following page is a list of criteria to aid you in selecting participants in a problem-solving situation.

Criteria for problem-solving meeting attenders

- *Knowledge of subject area involved in the problem.* The expertise required to develop a valid solution to the problem should be represented among the team membership.
- *Commitment to solving the problem.* Team members should have a vested interest in solving the problem.
- *Time to participate.* Each person must have time to participate in problem-solving activities.

- *Diversity of viewpoint.* The team must be able to look at a problem in different ways to avoid stereotyped thinking.
- *Expressiveness.* Team members must feel free to express facts, opinions, and feelings.
- *Open-mindedness.* Team members must be willing to listen to each other. This allows for the best solution when members are willing to change their minds when convinced by compelling arguments.

Choosing a meeting time

Certain days of the week and selected times of day are better than others for holding meetings. In order to have your participants present, on time, and ready to engage in the business of the meeting, give careful thought to your meeting time.

Considerations in choosing a meeting time include: your availability, participants' availability, facilities' availability, and preparation time required. First, look at preparation time required. Then check your availability and the availability of facilities. This will narrow the range of options. Finally, check with participants to ascertain their schedules. This should lead to a mutually satisfactory meeting time.

When choosing a time to meet, avoid late afternoons before a holiday or weekend, or early mornings following a day off. Be willing to be creative. For example, consider meeting at noon over a working lunch, or before the start of the official working day, with a continental breakfast.

Meetings of non-business groups such as civic associations or professional societies must meet outside normal working hours. They face more of a challenge to find an acceptable meeting time. These sessions will typically fall on a weekday evening. If you are part of a small group, explore the possibility of meeting at an unconventional time acceptable to all involved. For example, your group may meet from 9.00 to 11.00 on Saturday morning, 2.00 to 4.00 on Sunday afternoon, 6.00 to 7.30 on Wednesday morning, or 9.00 to 10.30 on Friday evening. Remember, if facilities are available and everyone is willing to meet, any time is acceptable.

Pick a time for your meetings

Use this worksheet to schedule or reschedule tentatively some of the meetings for which you are responsible. Don't arbitrarily eliminate unconventional times.

	Mon	Tues	Wed	Thur	Fri	Sat	Sun
6.00							
7.00							
8.00							
9.00							
10.00							
11.00							
12.00							
1.00							
2.00							
3.00							
4.00							
5.00							
6.00							
7.00							
8.00							
9.00							
10.00							
11.00							

Arranging facilities

The meeting room and its furnishings will contribute signifi-cantly to an effective meeting. When facilities are right, they go unnoticed. When they are inadequate or too elaborate, they can detract from the meeting.

On-site meeting rooms are usually convenient and low cost. This makes them attractive considerations. However, being convenient for participants also makes them convenient for interruptions. Occasionally, an on-site room will not be the right size for a particular meeting. Be willing to look elsewhere for a proper meeting place.

The need for participants to be physically comfortable should not be overlooked. If a meeting is to last over an hour, chairs should have cushions. Also, heating/cooling, lighting, and venti-lation should be adequate for the size of the group and activities planned.

A table is required only when it has a use (ie to write on, spread out maps, charts, computer printouts, etc). While tables are standard in most meeting rooms, consider your need. Perhaps a better room arrangement would be available without one.

When setting up the room, be guided by the communication needs for the type of meeting you plan to hold. As a rule of thumb, you want those talking to each other to maintain eye contact. Therefore, information meetings should have partici-pants facing the front of the room, while decision-making meetings should have participants facing each other. Examples of different room arrangements are shown on the following pages.

As you consider the selection of your meeting place, the checklist on the next page should prove helpful. The meeting arrangements checklist opposite will also help you to handle necessary arrangements.

Meeting room checklist
The following list summarises the key requirements for an acceptable meeting room. Use it to see if the potential meeting room will meet your needs.

Yes/No

————— 1. Is the room large enough to accommodate the participants comfortably and any planned audio-visual aids?

————— 2. Is there adequate lighting and ventilation? Can they be controlled within the meeting room?

————— 3. Is the room free from distractions and interruptions such as telephones, loud noises, or other activities?

————— 4. Is the room appropriately furnished? Are the chairs comfortable enough for the length of the meeting?

————— 5. Is the room conveniently located for participants?

————— 6. Is the cost of the room within budget?

————— 7. Is the room available at the time you need it?

Meeting arrangements checklist

The following list summarises typical meeting arrangements. Use it as a model for your meetings.

————— 1. Tables and chairs properly arranged for the type of meeting to be conducted.

————— 2. Table name cards for participants (if everyone is not well acquainted).

————— 3. Audi-visual equipment as required:

   (a) Chalkboard or flipchart
   (b) Overhead projector
   (c) Other – film projector, slide projector, video, audio cassette recorder.

————— 4. Refreshments as appropriate.

————— 5. Scheduled breaks for meetings longer than one and a half hours.

Sample room arrangement for information meeting

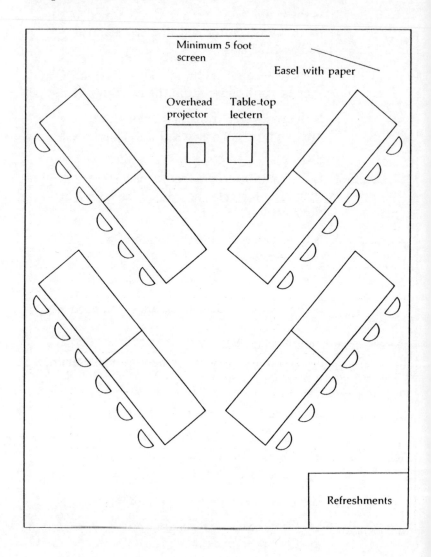

Sample room arrangement for information meeting

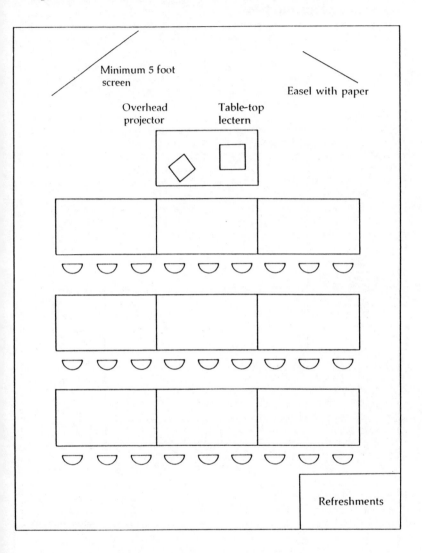

Sample room arrangement for either information or decision-making meeting

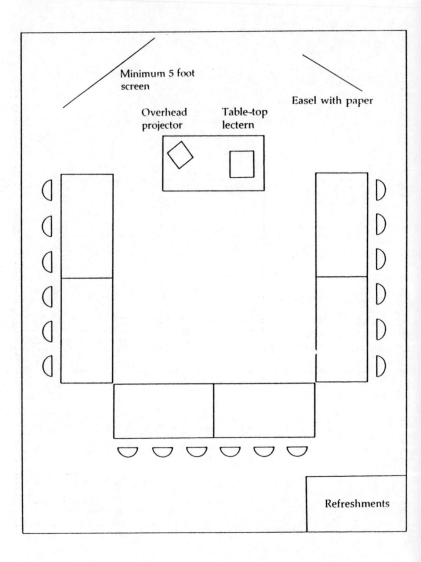

Sample room arrangement for decision-making meeting

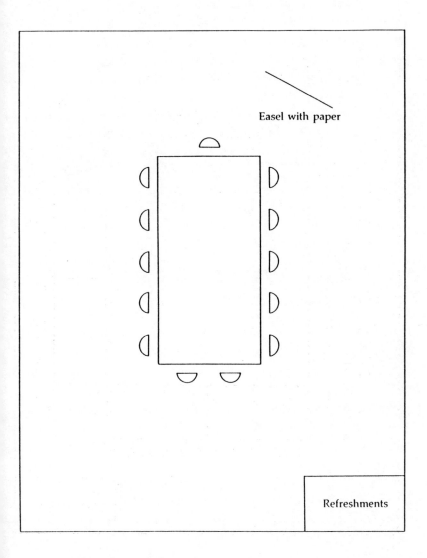

Easel with paper

Refreshments

Sample room arrangement for decision-making meeting

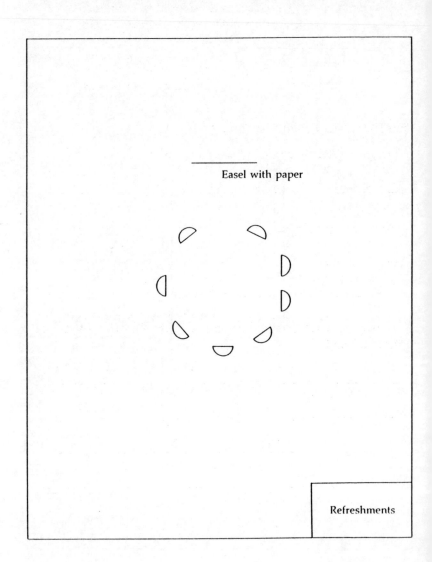

_____ 6. An appropriate smoking policy. If possible, keep a no smoking rule. If smoking is allowed, designate a smoking section and provide ashtrays.

_____ 7. All necessary materials available, such as handouts, notebooks, paper, and pencils.

Worksheet for planning a meeting

1. *Objective.* What key results do you want to achieve?

_____

_____

_____

_____

2. *Timing.* How long should the meeting last? When is the best time to hold it?

_____

_____

_____

_____

3. *Participants.* Who should attend? Be sure to include those with authority to decide, those whose commitment is needed, and those who need to know.

_____

_____

_____

_____

4. *Agenda.* What items should be dealt with? Who is responsible for preparing and distributing the agenda? How will participants help in developing the agenda?

_____

_____

_____

_____

5. *Physical arrangements.* What facilities and equipment are required? How should the meeting room be arranged?

_____

_____

_____

_____

6. *Role assignments.* What role assignments need to be made? For example, minute-taker, secretary, timekeeper, and discussion moderator.

_____

_____

_____

_____

7. *Evaluation method.* How will the meeting be evaluated in order to improve the next session?

_____

_____

_____

_____

Check what you learned in Chapter 2

Consider the following statements and mark each one true or false, based on the material in Chapter 2.

True/False

_____ 1. A meeting is the best way to disseminate information to a large group.

_____ 2. An individual can normally solve a problem better than a group.

_____ 3. Some meetings should be conducted without the benefit of an agenda.

_____ 4. Staff meetings usually have published agendas.

_____ 5. An agenda is an effective means of controlling the discussion in a meeting.

_____ 6. Everyone who wants to attend should be invited to meetings.

_____ 7. Invited participants should either contribute to the meeting or gain from having attended.

_____ 8. The wishes of participants need not be considered when choosing a meeting time.

_____ 9. Meeting facilities can affect a participant's attitude.

_____ 10. Participants' physical comfort is an important consideration when choosing a meeting place.

_____ 11. Desired communication patterns influence the arrangement of the meeting room.

_____ 12. A classroom style arrangement is best for a problem-solving meeting.

_____ 13. Name cards are a good idea if everyone is not well acquainted.

_____ 14. Every meeting room should have a stated smoking policy.

_____ 15. A conference table is required in every meeting room.

See page 94 for recommended responses.

CHAPTER 3
Conducting Meetings

The meeting leader's role

The meeting leader must focus the energy and attention of participants and keep them moving towards the meeting's objectives. This is a multifaceted task which can be better understood by breaking a meeting into three major components.

The major components of a meeting

- *Content.* The information, knowledge, experience, opinions, ideas, myths, attitudes, and expectations that participants bring to the meeting.
- *Interaction.* The way participants work together while processing the meeting's content. Includes feelings, attitudes, and expectations that bear on cooperation, listening, participation, trust, and openness.
- *Structure.* The way in which both information and participants are organised to achieve the meeting's purpose.

An effective leader is attentive to each of the above meeting components. The meeting leader's role is to monitor progress and provide direction. In some meetings participants help to provide direction. This makes the leader's job easier. In other meetings the leader is required to provide most of the direction.

To be an effective leader you must be able to analyse each situation, decide what is needed to move forward, and take the necessary action to achieve the objectives. In the next section is an outline of activities in each of the component areas that may be appropriate during a meeting.

In the sections that follow you will receive specific instructions on techniques for structuring decision-making meetings and for handling effective interaction.

Activities involved in conducting meetings

The leader's role is to monitor the activity in each key component area and provide the missing elements required to move the group towards the meeting's objectives.

Content

- Initiate action
- Keep on topic
- Elicit information
- Compare/ Contrast viewpoints
- Summarise
- Test for decision
- Develop action plans

Interaction

- Monitor participation
- Encourage participation
- Model supportive behaviour
- Encourage building/ supporting
- Encourage differing/ confronting
- Facilitate conflict resolution
- Explore reactions and feelings
- Facilitate feedback among members

Structure

- Develop agenda
- State objectives
- Manage time
- Use procedures and techniques for:
  - recording/ displaying data
  - analysing data
  - generating alternatives
  - making decisions
- Make role assignments
- Develop ground rules

Structuring decision-making meetings

Decision-making meetings need structure to keep attention focused on the problem. Structure will help to maintain the discipline of problem-solving. For example, some participants may come to the meeting with solutions to propose. When this happens, work will be required to concentrate on the process of problem-solving. The best way to do this is to follow the *rational decision process.*

Rational decision process

- Study/discuss/analyse the situation
- Define the problem
- Set an objective
- State imperatives and desirables
- Generate alternatives
- Establish evaluation criteria
- Evaluate alternatives
- Choose among alternatives

When using the rational decision process you first need to spend time discussing the situation and defining the problem. This ensures that you are dealing with the right problem. Then, state an objective (ie the end result you want to accomplish). If imperatives exist, list them along with the desirable features of your eventual outcome. If there are mutually exclusive imperatives, each must be reconciled or you cannot solve the problem. Obviously, you want as few imperatives as possible. Next, generate alternatives, through whatever method you choose. Then set up some evaluation criteria, evaluate the alternatives against those criteria, and make a decision. A straightforward, orderly eight-step process.

Generating alternatives

Alternatives can be generated in several different ways. The most common is by open discussion. Two procedures will probably produce more alternatives and reflect greater creativity. They are *Brainstorming* and *nominal group technique*.

● *Brainstorming.* This is a free form process that taps into the creative potential of a group through association. Power of association is a two-way current. When a group member voices an idea, this invites other ideas by stimulating the associative power of all other members.

● *Nominal group technique.* This structured process has group members write down individual ideas, then report them to the group. It minimises conformity while maximising participation.

When choosing between these techniques, consider whether or not participants have enough experience to deal with the information you seek. If they know the subject, nominal group technique gives you an orderly method for getting it reported to the group. If they are unfamiliar with the subject, brainstorming will create potential alternatives. The procedures for each are given on the next page.

Caution. Do not permit evaluative discussion during the time you are generating alternatives.

Brainstorming procedures

● List all ideas offered by group members.
● Do not evaluate or judge ideas at this time.
● Do not discuss ideas except perhaps briefly to clarify understanding.
● Welcome 'blue sky' ideas. It is always easier to eliminate than to accumulate.
● Repetition is all right. Don't waste time sorting out duplication.
● Encourage quantity. The more ideas, the greater the likelihood of a useful one.

- Don't be too anxious to close this phase. When a plateau is reached, let things rest and then start again.

Nominal group technique procedures

- Each member writes out ideas in response to the question presented to the group.
- Invite the group to report what they have written, one idea at a time. List the ideas in front of the group.
- Members should add new ideas to the list after the group has finished reporting.
- Continue the process until all ideas are reported.

Choosing among alternatives

There are several decision-making procedures available to groups during meetings. These tend to be either individual or group centred. Individual centred procedures are consolidations of individual choices, while group centred procedures rely on discussion and agreement. There is also a nominal group technique that falls between these two options. The following decision-making methods are most commonly used in meetings:

- *Voting.* This form of decision-making is appropriate in larger groups. It should be used in small groups only as a back-up style, or when the decision being made is inconsequential. A minimum number of positive votes can be set higher than simple majority to reduce the level of resistance to the decision made.

- *Consensus.* This form of decision-making maximises the support of the decision by participants. By nature, it is a highly interactive process and tends to produce quality decisions with a high level of commitment.

Nominal group technique. This form of decision-making is a reiterative process that minimises conformity and moves participants to decisions which they can support. The steps involved are:

- After discussion of the alternatives, members rate each on a numerical scale against agreed criteria.
- Ratings are reported for each alternative and added together.
- Alternatives with low total ratings are dropped from the list.
- The alternatives remaining are again discussed, rated and summarised. Those receiving the lowest ratings are dropped from the list.
- This process is repeated as required until a clear group choice remains.

Criteria based rating. After agreeing appropriate criteria such as feasibility, availability, and affordability, each alternative is rated on either a numerical scale or a low, moderate, high scale. Ratings can be achieved either by discussion or by consolidating individual ratings.

Criterion based ranking. Rather than rating alternatives on a scale, they can be ranked from high to low on each criterion. The rankings can be done either by discussion or by consolidating individual rankings. (The least desirable method is to vote on rank orders.)

Criterion based paired comparison. If often facilitates decision-making to limit the process to a series of decisions between two alternatives. This can be done by pairing all available alternatives, then consolidating the results of each decision. The sample paired comparison matrix on page 44 simplifies the process. Each decision can then be made either by discussion until agreement is reached or voting.

Decisions by consensus
Consensus is a decision process that makes full use of available resources and resolves conflicts creatively. Consensus is sometimes difficult to reach, so not every group decision can be made in this way. Complete unanimity is not the goal – it is rarely achieved. But each individual should be able to accept the group's decision on the basis of logic and feasibility. When all group members feel this way a consensus has been reached and the

judgement may be entered as the group's decision. The following are some guidelines to achieve consensus:

1. Avoid arguing for your position. Present your position as lucidly and logically as possible, but listen to the other members' reactions and consider them carefully.
2. Do not assume that someone must win and someone must lose when discussions reach stalemate. Instead, look for the next most acceptable alternative for all parties.
3. Do not change your mind simply to avoid conflict. When agreement seems to come too quickly and easily, be suspicious. Explore the reasons and be sure everyone accepts the solution for basically similar or complementary reasons. Yield only to positions that have objective and logically sound foundations.
3. Avoid conflict-reducing techniques such as voting, averaging, and bargaining. When a dissenting member finally agrees, don't feel that he or she must be rewarded by being allowed to 'win' on some later point.
5. Differences of opinion are natural and expected. Seek them out and try to involve everyone in the decision process. Disagreements can help the group's decision because, with a wide range of information and opinions, there is a greater chance that the group will hit upon a more adequate solution.

Worksheets are given overleaf.

Sample criterion based rating worksheet

Alternatives	Criteria			
	1.	2.	3.	4.
1.				
2.				
3.				
4.				
5.				
6.				
7.				
8.				
9.				
10.				

Note. Evaluations can be either on a subjective scale such as High, Moderate, Low; an objective scale such as 1 to 5 or 1 to 10; or actual values can be used, such as price, weight or delivery time.

List appropriate criteria across the top. (Usually one to four will be sufficient). Decide upon a procedure for deciding a group evaluation of each alternative on each criterion – such as consensus, voting, or averaging individual ratings. Final choice will be the alternative that rates the best on the most criteria.

Sample criterion based ranking worksheet

Alternatives	Participants' rankings							Consolidated ranking
	1.	2.	3.	4.	5.	6.	Total	
1.								
2.								
3.								
4.								
5.								
6.								
7.								
8.								
9.								
10.								

List participants' individual rankings and then add across to get a total of individual rankings. The alternative with the lowest total is ranked '1' in the consolidated ranking and so on, until the one with the largest total is ranked last.

Sample criterion based paired comparison worksheet

		Alternatives										Number of Xs
Yes = X No = Blank		1.	2.	3.	4.	5.	6.	7.	8.	9.	10.	
Alternatives	1.											
	2.											
	3.											
	4.											
	5.											
	6.											
	7.											
	8.											
	9.											
	10.											
	Number of blanks:											
	Number of Xs:											
	TOTAL											
	Priority											

List each alternative twice – on a horizontal line and the corresponding vertical line. Compare alternative 1 with alternative 2. If 1 rates higher put an 'X' in the box; if 2 rates higher leave blank. Continue across comparing 1 with all the other alternatives then go to the next line and repeat the process until all pairs have been compared. Count the Xs across for each alternative and enter the number in the far right column, then transfer the totals to the line at the bottom of the chart labelled 'number of Xs'. Count the blanks down and enter in the appropriate line at the bottom. Add the number of Xs and blanks for each alternative and enter in the line marked 'Total'. The largest total will be the number 1 choice, next highest number 2, etc. In case of a tie, go back and compare the two again.

Stimulating discussion

The success of any discussion depends upon participation. An atmosphere of free exchange can be created only when participants see that a mutual sharing of opinions and ideas is welcome. The skilful use of questions will encourage discussion.

You should be constantly alert for cues from the group that suggest problems. If participants begin to fidget, look bored, or show by their expressions that they don't understand, or disagree, you should ask questions to find out what is going on.

Questions are of four basic types:

- *General* which elicit a broad range of potential responses.
- *Specific* which focus on an idea leaving a limited range of responses.
- *Overhead* which are asked of the group allowing volunteers to respond.
- *Direct* which are asked of a selected individual.

From *Management by Objectives and Results for Business and Industry* by George L Morrisey (Addison-Wesley Publishing Co, 1977). Used by permission of the author.

General and *overhead* questions are less threatening and therefore better to start a discussion. *Direct* and *specific* questions are best used after participants become comfortable with group discussion.

The following examples provide some useful guidelines for generating discussion.

1. **Ask for feelings and opinions**
   Use a method of asking questions that will help people to express their ideas, draw people out, and encourage discussion. For example:

   - What is your reaction to ...?
   - How do you feel about ...?
   - What is your thinking on ...?
   - What brings you to conclude that ...?
   - What are some other ways to get at ...?
   - What prompted your decision to ...?
   - How did you happen to learn that ...?
   - How did you feel when you found out that ...?
   - Would you say that ...?

2. **Paraphrase**
   One way to help people reach mutual understanding is to paraphrase, that is, to ask one person to repeat what someone else said and to state what that person meant:

   - Are you asking me to ...?
   - Let me see if I understand your position. Are you saying that ...?
   - I'm not sure I understand. Are you saying that ...?
   - Before we go on, let me paraphrase what I think you are proposing.
   - Let me restate your last point to see if I understand.
   - What I am hearing is ... Is that right?
   - Before you go on, do you mean that ...?

3. Encourage participation

Sometimes people tend to hold back. They can be encouraged to participate by such questions as:

- Charles, how do you feel about this?
- Mary, how would you answer John's questions?
- Before we go on, I'd like to hear from Bill on this.
- We have heard from everyone but Jane. Jane, what is your feeling on this?
- We haven't heard from Jack yet. Jack, how do you feel about this?

4. Ask for a summary

- A lot of good ideas have been presented in the last few minutes. Will someone please summarise the major points before we go on?
- I have heard a number of proposals. Will someone summarise what has been agreed?
- It is clear Jim does not agree. Jim, will you summarise your major objections?
- I have lost track. Will someone summarise what has been done so far?

5. Ask for clarification

- I didn't understand that last comment. What would you do if ...?
- The examples you gave concern weekday operations. Do they also apply to weekends ...?
- I saw Maureen shaking her head. Maureen, would it help if we took a minute to explain how these new instructions apply to your department?
- It is still not clear to me. What do I do when ...?

6. Ask for examples

- Dorothy, will you give some examples of what you mean?
- John, can you expand on that? I'm not sure I understand.

7. Test for consensus

- It seems that we have come to agreement on this issue. Let me ask for a show of hands on this. Does everyone accept the idea that ...?
- Glenda, is that your feeling too ...?
- Before we go on to the next issue, let me check to make sure that we have all agreed to ...

8. Initiate action

- How do you think we should ...?
- Frank, how would you suggest that we proceed on this?
- I'd like some suggestions on possible ways to get started. Peter, how would you propose we get started?

9. Explore an idea in more detail

- What other ways could we approach this problem?
- Are there other things we should consider?
- Oliver, what would you add to what has been said?

10. Do a quick survey

- Let's see a show of hands. How many are in favour of this proposal?
- Beverly, why don't you ask the others how they feel about your proposal?
- How does everybody feel about this? Let's start with Louis.

11. Suggest a break

- We have been working on this problem for about an hour. I propose we take a 10-minute break.

12. Suggest a procedure

- I noticed that Carla has done most of the talking on this issue. I suggest we go round the table to see how others feel.
- Would it help if we put the agenda items in order of importance before we started?

13. Suggest they try something

- Bridget, I don't think you heard what Winnie was trying to say. Why don't you tell us what you think her argument is before you state your objections.
- Let's go round the table so that everyone gets a chance to comment on this.

14. Stop the action and ask the group to talk about something

- Let's stop the discussion for a few minutes. I think it might help if each of us told the group what he or she is feeling – right now.

15. Share your feelings

- I feel you are not giving Harry a chance to explain his position.
- I'm getting nowhere. I think we should take this problem up next week when we have more facts. How do the rest of you feel?

16. Reflect what you think someone is feeling

- George, I get the impression that you are not satisfied

with my answer. Is that right?

- Kim's comments tell me that he needs to ask some questions on this – is that right, Kim?

17. Be supportive

- Let's give Tony a chance to tell us how he sees the problem.
- Dave, you've had your say. Now it's Harold's turn. Give him a chance to explain.

18. Question assumptions

- Your proposal assumes that unless we use threats, they won't cooperate. Is that right?
- Your suggestion assumes that we cannot meet the schedule. Is that right?
- Your objection assumes that we will not get promised deliveries. Is this a good assumption?

19. Check targets or orientation

- Are we asking the right question?
- Are these the most important goals?
- Is this the best way to get their cooperation?
- Is this the only way to get it done?

20. Confront differences

- Nick, you haven't said so but it is clear to me that you don't agree. Is that right?
- Martha, you seem to be holding back on this. Is there something here you disagree with?

21. Role reversal

- Why don't you take the role of a customer for a few

minutes. Now, as a customer, how would you react to this proposal?
- Pretend you are the district manager for a moment. How would he react to this proposal?
- How would you feel if I treated you like that?

22. Look into the future

- If we did it this way, what is the worst thing that could happen?
- If it doesn't work, what have we lost?
- If it works, how will it affect next week's schedule?

23. Focus on action choice

- We have considered every possibility, we must choose from these three alternatives.
- We have discussed both sides carefully. It's time we made a choice.

Things to avoid

1. *Unanswerable questions*
   Be sure that the questions you ask can be answered by the group or by some member of the group.

2. *Questions of simple assent or dissent*
   Unless followed by other questions of the Why, When, Where, How, What, Who sort, a yes or no answer leads nowhere.

3. *Vague, indefinite, ambiguous questions*
   To get satisfactory answers, you must ask good questions. Sometimes you may need to rephrase your question or break it down into subquestions if not immediately understood. Above all, never try to play with words or trap a participant into an incorrect or misleading answer.

4. *Witnessbox interrogation*

   You may have to ask a participant questions in the interest of clarification, but remember that you are not out to prove anything. Your conduct should never be that of a courtroom cross-examination where the person answering feels threatened.

Effective use of questions

Select a response from the right-hand column which correctly describes what you would do in the situations described in the left-hand column. Write the letter corresponding to your choice on the line in front of the number of the situation. (It is all right to repeat a response.)

Situation	Response
___ 1. You want to stimulate discussion.	(a) Ask each participant to summarise the other's position.
___ 2. You want to cut off discussion.	(b) Ask for feedback from the group.
___ 3. You want to bring a participant into the discussion.	(c) Ask the group a general question.
___ 4. Two participants are engaging in side conversation.	(d) Ask an individual a specific question.
___ 5. You are asked a question you are not sure you can answer.	(e) Ask the group a specific question.
___ 6. You want to test the level of support for a point of view.	(f) Ask an individual a general question.
___ 7. Two participants are debating a point. Everyone else is watching.	(g) Ask the group for a summary.

____ 8. Discussion has been going on for some time. You're unclear of progress.

(h) Ask an individual to summarise the discussion.

____ 9. Two people have been debating a point without much progress.

(i) Direct the question back to the group.

____ 10. You would like to know if you have been an effective leader.

(j) None of the above.

See page 94 for recommended responses.

Handling difficult situations

Because meetings depend on interaction, it is inevitable that problem situations will occur. Sometimes problems originate with people, sometimes with procedures or logic. In any case, it is the responsibility of the leader to provoke discussion of the most profitable kind, to make sure participation is distributed among members of the group, and to keep the discussion heading in the right direction.

The following are examples of difficult situations and how to handle them.

A person who tends to dominate the discussion

A talkative participant must not be permitted to dominate the discussion. General participation is essential to the success of a meeting, since the purpose is to bring out different points of view. Sometimes a person may assume a dominant role because of being more experienced or more senior than others present. Often, if that is the case, others will sit back and give up the floor. When this happens, the leader should use direct questions to draw out other participants. It is helpful to avoid looking at the senior person when presenting a question, thus making it difficult for that person to get your attention.

If nothing else is effective, a private chat with the individual during a coffee break may help.

A person who wants to argue

This individual may be a know-all, full of misinformation, or a quibbler who takes delight in crossing the leader. In any case, the leader must keep a cool head. By using questions, the leader can draw out such a person, giving him or her an opportunity to make foolish or far-fetched statements, and then turn the person over to the group. Usually, such a person irritates the group and unfavourable opinions will be expressed and may bring temporary silence. Subsequently, the leader may use direct questions to other participants as a means of maintaining the balance.

Often an argumentative person will recognise what has happened and not present further problems. However, if the person is insensitive, the leader may have to be very direct, pointing out that the quibbling is interrupting the progress of the meeting and is a waste of valuable time. The leader should then immediately turn to another person with a question to take the discussion forward.

A person who starts another meeting with neighbours

This problem is more likely to occur in a larger group. It may be the result of a talkative individual's need to speak when unable to address the group as a whole, or it may be the result of a more cautious thinker's desire to try out an idea before bringing it before the entire group. Side conversations are inevitable in a typical meeting and are apt to be brief. They become a problem only if prolonged.

One technique is to invite the individual to share with everyone what is being said. Another way to handle this situation is simply to be quiet and look at the offending person. Generally, this will bring the meeting back to order.

Certain problems originate, not with people who talk too much, but with those who talk too little or not at all. Here are some to look out for:

A person who is timid or lacking in self-confidence

Whether such a person feels uncertain because of inexperience or is simply unwilling to speak due to embarrassment, the leader should ask a question in an area where the reluctant individual can speak with conviction. Usually, once the ice has been broken and anxiety dissolved, the individual will become a thoughtful contributor.

A person who is antagonistic or sceptical

Sometimes people are antagonistic to the meeting, or the leader, or sceptical about the use of time. Usually, such attitudes can be traced either to previous experiences with meetings or a leader's lack of skill in opening the meeting (clarifying its objectives) and conducting the discussion. If meetings have been merely management briefing sessions, at which the expression of opinion was invited but not really desired – it is the responsibility of the leader to clarify the real purpose of the meeting.

If, on the other hand, the antagonism is of a more personal nature, it requires the utmost sensitivity and tact to make the individual feel there is genuine interest in what he or she has to say. Here, as in other aspects of interpersonal relations, good will and objectivity must be readily evident.

A person who attempts to get an opinion instead of give one

Experience has shown some people that some managers do not really want ideas and prefer to be asked for their own. Such people will reply to questions with another question. Confronted with this situation, the best technique is to refer the question back to the group and then back to the one who asked it.

The following situations are impersonal. They call for a different kind of response.

Establishing and holding the interest of the group

It is essential to engage attention in the opening statement and then motivate the group to respond. Visual aids should be used as the discussion progresses. Case studies for group analysis are also effective. If response lags, change the approach. *Keep things moving.*

Voice can be an effective tool to help regain interest. If interest is waning, speak more loudly, more rapidly and with more feeling. Usually, this will stimulate the energy of the meeting.

Starting a discussion when necessary

Ask questions demanding consideration of the problem from an unusual point of view. Use cases, real or hypothetical. Call for specific experiences, ideas, or opinions from group members.

Keeping up with the pace of the discussion

Try to crystallise statements into phrases which can be recorded quickly. Ignore statements not relevant to the topic. Pursue an important line of enquiry with direct questions.

Handling touchy subjects

Anticipate what touchy subjects may arise and face them squarely. If they are not truly relevant to the subject under discussion, point that out, referring to the objectives of the meeting. If they are pertinent, remain neutral, insisting on an objective consideration of the question. Do not promise to get action from management, but only to report the conclusions or findings.

Developing discussion and avoiding superficiality

Be prepared to cite specific cases and facts for consideration if they are not forthcoming from group members. Call on individuals known to have had specific relevant experience, past or present. Encourage members to take issue with trends or statements to avoid the 'bandwagon'. Encourage original thought. Probe opinions for factual or conceptual causes. Do not permit oversimplification of anything.

Rank your choices for each of the following situations. Place a '1' next to the solution you most favour, a '2' by the one you next favour etc, until you place a '4' by the one you favour least.

1. You arrive early and find the meeting room is arranged differently from what you would like although you feel you could just about manage with the present arrangement.

   ☐ (a) Phone the section responsible for the room and have it rearranged.
   ☐ (b) Rearrange the room yourself.
   ☐ (c) Wait until participants begin to arrive and have someone help to rearrange things.
   ☐ (d) Leave the room as it is and complain later to the responsible section.

2. You expect 10 participants at a 9.00 am meeting. It is 9.05 and only eight participants are present. No one advised you of plans to arrive late.

   ☐ (a) Begin the meeting with those present.
   ☐ (b) Phone the two absentees to see if they are coming.
   ☐ (c) Wait another five minutes and then begin.
   ☐ (d) Ask those present to vote on whether to begin now or later.

3. Some participants are not contributing to the meeting although they appear to be attentive.

   ☐ (a) Monitor the situation to see if it continues.
   ☐ (b) Ask a non-contributing participant for an opinion or reaction.
   ☐ (c) Ask the non-contributing participants why they are not involved.
   ☐ (d) Do nothing – they'll speak up if they want to.

4. You want discussion on a topic but no one is talking.

   ☐ (a) Ask a general question of the group.
   ☐ (b) Ask a specific question on an individual.
   ☐ (c) As for feedback on why no one is talking.
   ☐ (d) Adjourn the meeting due to lack of interest.

5. You notice, through non-verbal signs, that the interest level of the group is fading.

   ☐ (a) Shorten your agenda and adjourn the meeting.
   ☐ (b) Take a five-minute break.
   ☐ (c) Speak more loudly and in a more animated fashion.
   ☐ (d) Try to start a discussion.

6. You get a question you can't answer.

   ☐ (a) Redirect the question to the group.
   ☐ (b) Ignore the question.
   ☐ (c) Ask the person who asked the question why he or she asked it.
   ☐ (d) Admit you don't know the answer and move on.

7. A participant is using too much time talking about an item that is not on the agenda.

   ☐ (a) Interrupt and point out the need to get back to the agenda.
   ☐ (b) Do nothing and hope the meeting makes some progress.
   ☐ (c) Ask participants if they want to discuss the subject.
   ☐ (d) Tell the participant the topic will be taken up at the end of the meeting if there is enough time.

8. The group is getting away from the objective of the meeting.

   ☐ (a) Let things go as long as everyone seems interested.
   ☐ (b) Interrupt and bring the group back to the agenda.
   ☐ (c) Interrupt and vote on whether or not to continue this discussion.
   ☐ (d) Take a break so participants can continue the discussion in their own time and reconvene when it is over.

9. It is time for a scheduled break. When you announce the break your boss, who is a participant in the meeting, says it isn't necessary.

   ☐ (a) Confront your boss as to who's running the meeting.
   ☐ (b) Cancel the break and continue the meeting.
   ☐ (c) Take a break and let your boss continue the meeting.
   ☐ (d) Ask the group if it wants to take a break.

10. Two people, sitting together, keep whispering to each other. It has been going on for some time. You find it distracting.

   ☐ (a) Ask them to share their discussion with the group.
   ☐ (b) Ask them a content-related question to see if they've been listening.
   ☐ (c) Stop talking and look at them.
   ☐ (d) Ignore it and hope they finish soon.

See page 95 for recommended responses.

Managing conflict

Interpersonal conflict in meetings is not necessarily bad. In fact, it can be healthy when handled properly. Therefore, the question is not how to eliminate conflict but how to capitalise on its constructive aspects. In many instances interpersonal differences, competition, rivalry, and other forms of conflict contribute to the effectiveness of the meeting. A moderate level of conflict may have these constructive consequences:

- Increase motivation and energy to carry out a task.
- Increase innovative thinking through a greater diversity of viewpoints.
- Increase understanding of a position on an issue by forcing the advocate of that position to articulate and support it with facts.
- Increase understanding of opposing positions on an issue by being forced to listen and then working to integrate diverse positions to achieve consensus

When everyone is doing his or her best, conflict is natural. What is best for one department won't necessarily be the best for others. Therefore, conflict management becomes a primary skill for conducting effective meetings.

What causes conflict?

Conflict develops when participants in the meeting become assertive while presenting their points of view. It often occurs when individuals come to the meeting with preconceived ideas about the outcome of the discussion rather than considering what conditions must be satisfied in order to be acceptable to the group.

Conflict results from four classic conditions:

- Lack of communication
- Different perceptions
- Different values
- Different preferred outcomes

Since assertiveness is a necessary element in conflict, it is important to understand the conditions under which conflict is likely to occur:

- People tend to be more assertive when an issue is important to them.
- People tend to be more assertive when they feel confident of their knowledge or understanding of an issue.
- People tend to be more assertive when they sense that the course of the discussion is going contrary to their preferred course.
- People tend to be less assertive when the opposition is viewed as possessing more power and they feel that power might be used for retaliation.
- Some people are naturally more assertive than others.

Cooperation is another element that needs to be considered when dealing with conflict. Cooperation hinges on three primary issues:

- People tend to be more cooperative when they respect the opposition.
- People tend to be more cooperative when they value their relationship with the opposition.
- People tend to be more cooperative when they recognise that the opposition is needed to help implement a satisfactory outcome.

The model below shows some common responses to conflict as a function of different levels of assertiveness and cooperation.

Responses to conflict

HIGH ASSERTIVENESS	COMPETITION	COLLABORATION
LOW ASSERTIVENESS	AVOIDANCE	ACCOMMODATION
	LOW COOPERATION	HIGH COOPERATION

Competition. The upper left quadrant of the model above says, 'I'm confident of my knowledge. Winning is the name of the game.'

Collaboration. The upper right quadrant represents high assertiveness, but with the realisation that things need to be resolved in a cooperative manner.

Accommodation. The lower right quadrant suggests accommodation. There may be times when an issue is unimportant, or there is a lack of knowledge, or perhaps apprehension about retaliation. These concerns might be coupled with a high regard for the other party. This leads to accommodation or doing what the other person wants.

Avoidance. Avoidance is reflected in the lower left quadrant. This can happen when time is needed to collect more information, or simply because there is no desire to face up to an issue.

There are logical explanations for each approach. Each may be appropriate at times. However, people tend to migrate to one style and stay there. Many do not differentiate situations. Some people are competitive by nature and go into every situation trying to win. Others tend to be cooperative and see every situation as an opportunity to make a deal. A few people never stand up for what they believe. Others avoid conflict at any price. The important consideration is that conflict is natural and does not need to be avoided.

Dealing with conflict

Five general ways for dealing with conflict in a meeting are listed below:

- *Confrontation.* Those involved exchange information about a situation and express their feelings openly. Under these conditions, problem-solving becomes a matter of working through differences based upon valid data. Consensus is the objective. Confrontation requires emotional and intellectual energy as well as a high degree of interpersonal skill.

- *Compromise.* Instead of working through confrontation, another approach is to split differences and reach a compromise satisfactory to the various parties. Often a compromise resolution will not meet the needs of an organisation.

- *Smoothing.* Instead of confronting issues it is possible to smooth them over. In these cases, the approach is, 'We are friends and shouldn't let this problem disrupt our relationship. Let's allow it to work itself out.' Unfortunately, when problems are smoothed over, they are not usually solved. They often become worse with time.

- *Use of power.* Conflict can be handled by using power (of knowledge or position) to force a solution that is satisfactory from one point of view. This occurs when a superior produces a unilateral resolution, for example.

- *Coalition.* Conflict can also be resolved by factions forming an alliance to force others to accept their position. The disadvantage of this approach is that other parties feel their wishes have not been taken into account and are therefore less motivated to carry out the decisions.

Research indicates that confrontation is the best approach to conflict resolution. Properly done, it preserves the best interests of those involved. In spite of widely different positions, people can engage in effective problem-solving under conditions of conflict if they are willing to be constructive about their differences.

It is also essential to have a back-up method of dealing with conflict (ie compromise, coalition, or use of power). This ensures that the group will reach a decision instead of smoothing over or avoiding important problems.

Handling confrontation in meetings

The following ideas should help you to handle confrontations in a positive way.

Clarify objectives
Conflict sometimes develops because participants' understanding of the meeting's objectives differs. Clarifying and reaching agreement on objectives is an important first step.

Strive for understanding

Often, when involved in argument, people do not listen carefully to the opposition's presentation; they are too busy formulating a rebuttal. As the meeting leader, you may find it necessary to stop the action and make sure that each party in a confrontation can state the opposing party's position and supporting reasons.

Focus on the rational

Emotional involvement is a natural part of confrontation. However, sound decisions cannot be reached when participants are too emotional. Therefore, for the benefit of the outcome, you should keep attention focused on rational consideration – facts, supporting reasons, potential problems if a certain course of action is followed etc.

Generate alternatives

What alternative solutions integrate the needs of the diverse points of view involved in the confrontation? This is a challenging part of the process. Participants often cannot see any alternative to their solution. This is where group members at neither extreme can become a resource to generate some reasonable alternatives.

Postpone the issue

Postponement can be an effective way to deal with conflict when you feel a party needs time to consider the arguments that have been presented. It works particularly well as a face-saving device. People sometimes find themselves in a position of having argued so strongly for a position that they cannot gracefully change, even after being convinced of the logic of a different position. Postponement gives a person time to work this out.

Use humour

If you can use humour well, it can reduce the emotional tension of confrontation. It can serve as a release and clear the way for more rational problem-solving.

Other approaches to handling conflict in meetings include:

- An acknowledgement of deadlines
- Involving everyone in the process
- Allowing time to think
- Taking a break
- Referring items to a subcommittee
- Allowing for expression of strong feelings
- Protecting the group from early closure.

When there is a disagreement between two groups on how to resolve a problem, you can stop the discussion and deal with the conflict in the following way. Ask each group member to indicate where he or she stands on the following scale:

FOR	5	4	3	2	1	0	1	2	3	4	5	AGAINST

When group members have indicated their positions, ask them to write their scores on a flipchart. Then, ask group members who are *for* a given position to explain why other members are *against* it. Do the same with the other group. Ask those who are *against* the position to explain why the others are *for* it. This (1) provides a quick way to get the issues to the surface, (2) gets all pros and cons out in the open, (3) ensures that one group is listening and understands what the other group is saying and why. Finally, involve those who are neutral on the issue to offer alternatives which integrate the needs of those *for* and those *against*.

Conflict should not be avoided in meetings. It is a natural outcome of strongly held points of view. However, it must be contained and focused on resolution.

All conflict can be resolved. Not that it always will – but it can. Most often it is resolved through some communication. One expert estimates that 70 per cent of conflict can be handled by simply using clear communication. Twenty per cent will require negotiation. And the remaining 10 per cent can be resolved through arbitration or the use of a third party.

Rate yourself as a meeting leader

Tick yes or no to each of the following questions based on how you act (or would act) as a meeting leader. Be honest.

Yes   *No*

___ ___ 1. Do I have clear objectives for the meeting?

___ ___ 2. Am I selective about the invited participants?

___ ___ 3. Do I prepare an agenda and distribute it in advance of the meeting?

___ ___ 4. Do I arrive early enough to check the arrangements?

___ ___ 5. Do I start the meeting promptly regardless of who is present?

___ ___ 6. Do I follow the agenda?

___ ___ 7. Do I manage time and conclude the meeting as scheduled?

___ ___ 8. Do I elicit everyone's participation?

___ ___ 9. Do I help in the resolution of conflict?

___ ___ 10. Do I maintain proper control of the discussion?

___ ___ 11. Do I summarise decisions at the end of the meeting and clarify any action to be taken?

___ ___ 12. Do I prepare and distribute minutes of the meeting?

___ ___ 13. Do I request evaluative feedback from participants?

___ ___ 14. Do I take agreed action?

___ ___ 15. Do I follow up on action to be taken by others?

Being a productive participant

Everyone is a meeting participant at one time or another. An effective meeting depends on productive participants. As a participant, you are in a position to make a significant contribution to the success of meetings you attend. All you need is a tactful way to ask questions and offer suggestions.

A productive participant demonstrates all the behaviour previously mentioned for successful meetings. This includes being on time, not carrying on side conversations, being willing to ask questions, paying attention, listening, and staying involved. Other helpful things you can do as a participant include:

- Supporting useful ideas from the leader or other participants
- Judging the merit of ideas presented and not being distracted by delivery styles
- Delaying any judgement until the full idea has been presented
- Not allowing environmental conditions to distract you, such as noise or uncomfortable conditions
- Taking well-organised notes.

A good meeting participant

- Prepares for the meeting

- Contributes ideas to the discussion

- Listens to the ideas of others

- Considers the problem objectively

- Contributes to the orderly conduct of the meeting

- Provides feedback to the meeting leader

- Carries out agreed action.

Rate yourself as a meeting participant
Tick yes or no to each of the following questions based on how you participate in meetings. Be honest.

Effective Meeting Skills

Yes   *No*

____   ____   1. Do I usually know the purpose of the meetings I attend?

____   ____   2. Do I have a clear understanding of my role in meetings attended?

____   ____   3. Do I confirm my attendance in advance of the meeting?

____   ____   4. Do I complete required preparation such as looking up information or studying proposals?

____   ____   5. Do I arrive at meetings before they are scheduled to begin?

____   ____   6. Do I engage in side conversations while the meeting is in progress?

____   ____   7. Do I leave meetings for reasons such as non-emergency telephone calls?

____   ____   8. Do I ask questions when I am not sure about something?

____   ____   9. Am I usually open to the ideas of others?

____   ____   10. Am I a good listener?

____   ____   11. Do I actively participate in discussions when there is something worthwhile to contribute?

____   ____   12. Do I help others to stay on the subject?

____   ____   13. Following meetings, do I take agreed action?

____   ____   14. Do I contribute to improving meetings by giving feedback to the people who conduct them either by a note, phone call, or visit?

____   ____   15. Following meetings, do I inform appropriate people who did not attend about what was discussed and the outcome?

Check what you learned in Chapter 3

Answer each of the following questions based on material presented in Chapter 3.

1. The three major components of a meeting are:

   1. _____

   2. _____

   3. _____

2. The reason for following a structured decision process is:

   ☐ (a) To use the synergy of group interaction
   ☐ (b) To make it easier to run the meeting
   ☐ (c) To give everyone an equal opportunity to participate.

3. Two techniques for generating alternatives were presented – *Brainstorming* and *nominal group technique*. Under what conditions would you choose one rather than the other?

   _____

   _____

   _____

4. Voting is the least common form of decision-making in meetings?

   ☐ True   ☐ False

5. Consensus decisions tend to be the highest quality decisions made by groups.

   ☐ True   ☐ False

6. Rankings and ratings are too complicated for use in meetings.

   ☐ True   ☐ False

7. Discussion can be generated by:

   ☐ (a) Asking general questions of the group
   ☐ (b) Asking general questions of individuals
   ☐ (c) Providing an authentic opportunity for participants
         to comment or ask questions
   ☐ (d) All of the above.

8. All disruptive behaviour should be dealt with in the meeting.

   ☐ True   ☐ False

9. Your voice can be an effective tool to help regain interest.

   ☐ True   ☐ False

10. Conflict is to be expected in decision-making meetings.

    ☐ True   ☐ False

11. Conflict usually results from:

    ☐ (a) Lack of communication
    ☐ (b) Petty differences
    ☐ (c) Different perceptions
    ☐ (d) Different preferred outcomes.

12. All conflict can be resolved.

    ☐ True   ☐ False

13. All conflict will be resolved.

    ☐ True   ☐ False

14. The participant's role is as important to effective meetings as
    the leader's role.

    ☐ True   ☐ False

15. What can a participant do to contribute to an effective meeting?

_____

_____

_____

See page 95 for recommended responses.

CHAPTER 4
Improving Meetings

How to improve meetings

Practice makes perfect only when you practise the right things. You have learned many ways to make meetings more effective. However, some additional issues must also be included to ensure maximum improvement.

The most important element in bringing about improvement is the motivation to improve. As a leader, you may have received feedback that your meetings lacked something. Or, you may have noticed that your meetings tend to drag on and accomplish little. Regardless of what brings you to the realisation that improvement is in order, nothing will change until you are motivated to make things happen.

The first step will be to single out the elements that need to be changed. This is where input from others is essential. The next few pages go into detail on how to have meetings evaluated. Once improvement areas have been identified, you need feedback on how best to handle them.

Finally, once you have developed a new set of actions it is important to try them. Following each trial, evaluate the meeting to see if the change has been effective. If so, go on to the next area that needs improvement. If not, try something else until you solve the problem.

Improvement model

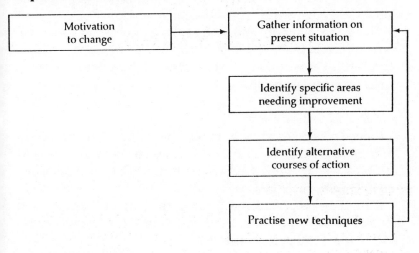

Meeting evaluation

Effective meetings occur when leaders and participants work to find a better way to get the job done. Participants come to a meeting with ideas, skills, knowledge, and experience. The leader's job is to create an environment where 'evaluation' becomes a normal part of the process.

Sources of evaluation

There are three potential sources for evaluating meetings:

- Self-evaluation by the leader
- Evaluation by a trained observer
- Evaluation by participants.

All should contribute to improving a meeting. However, evaluations by trained observers and participants tend to be broader in scope and more objective.

Self-evaluation by the leader
After a meeting is over, a leader should ask, 'How did I do?'

'Where did things go well, and why?' 'Where did I have problems, and why?' 'What would I do differently next time?'

This is the minimum evaluation to be considered. A leader will have impressions about things that went well and problem areas that were encountered. A few minutes reflecting on these experiences can be helpful.

Evaluation by a trained observer

A trained observer should be familiar with the ingredients of an effective meeting, skilled in making objective evaluations, and accomplished at giving feedback. It is difficult to find someone with all these qualifications.

A meeting observer usually sits in the back of the room and records notes on an evaluation form. Notes that follow a 'time-line' of the meeting are most helpful.

Following the meeting, the observer may either report to the group and invite discussion about how to improve the effectiveness of future meetings, or the trained observer may choose to report privately to the meeting leader to discuss improvement needs.

Evaluation by participants

Participants are an excellent resource for evaluation. They have feelings and reactions to meetings, events and leadership styles that others may not choose to acknowledge. An open discussion is usually the best way to get feedback from participants.

Timing of evaluations

There are three times when evaluation can take place: during the meeting, at the end of the meeting, or after the meeting has adjourned.

During the meeting

This evaluation need not be formal or complicated. During any meeting, the leader can be alert for signs that indicate something needs improving. These can be verbal or non-verbal; subtle or blunt. The simplest (and most effective) way is to stop the meeting and deal directly with what is happening.

Another way to assist an ongoing evaluation is to take time after a break and simply ask the group for comment:

- 'How is the meeting going so far?'
- 'What can we do to make our meeting more effective?'

Give participants time to think about the questions, then ask them to share their comments. Be prepared to listen carefully and respond to suggestions that are made.

At the end of the meeting
The evaluation forms on the following pages can be used to encourage people to examine their meetings. You may wish to select one of these or develop your own.

If you have time at the end of the meeting, it might be worthwhile to ask everyone to complete a form and list the scores on a flipchart for group discussion. The actual numbers are not of special importance. What is important is the opportunity to share perceptions of what is going on. The goal is to deal with items that can improve future meetings.

Caution should be exercised with end of meeting evaluations. Participants are often in a hurry so they do not take the time to do a quality evaluation. Be sure everyone has enough time to invest in the evaluation or defer it until later.

After the meeting
If you don't have time at the end of the meeting, these evaluation techniques are available:

- Distribute evaluation forms to participants asking them to complete and return them to you.
- Telephone a cross-section of the group and request a verbal evaluation of the meeting.
- Visit members of the meeting and ask them to evaluate it in a face-to-face discussion.

The benefits of an evaluation will be worthwhile if the following conditions exist:

- The leader wants to improve future meetings
- The leader receives honest input from evaluators
- Evaluators are candid in their assessment
- The leader receives feedback in a positive way
- The leader incorporates improvements into future meetings.

Setting meeting ground rules

Another suggestion to improve meeting effectiveness is to establish ground rules specifying how participants are to behave. These may either be set by the meeting leader or through discussion and agreement with participants. If the meeting is a one-off event, the unilateral approach is suggested. If the same participants meet regularly, a participative approach might be best.

Behaviour in meetings is based on experience. From these experiences, assumptions are made about what is proper. The way to deal with these assumptions is to set ground rules.

With a group that has met for several sessions, ask the question: 'What do we usually do in our meetings?' Then classify what is identified as either detracting from, or contributing to, the group's effectiveness. (Some things can be dropped as inconsequential.) Finally, develop ground rules to overcome detracting behaviour and reinforce contributing behaviour. Ground rules may be set in the content, interaction and/or structure areas.

Example of meeting ground rules

1. The meeting will begin on time.
2. Group members will help to set the meeting agenda.
3. Decisions will be made by consensus.
4. Conflict is acceptable, and sometimes desirable.
5. Expression of feelings and opinions is encouraged.

Meeting evaluation

1. To what extent did this meeting achieve its stated objectives?

   Not at all   1   2   3   4   5   6   7   8   9   Completely

2. To what extent did this meeting achieve your personal objectives?

   Not at all   1   2   3   4   5   6   7   8   9   Completely

3. Which parts of the meeting were most helpful to you?

   A _____

   B _____

   C _____

4. Which aspects were least helpful to you?

   A _____

   B _____

   C _____

5. What action will you be taking as a result of this meeting?

   _____

   _____

   _____

   _____

   _____

6. Other comments? Please use other side if necessary.

   _____

   _____

   _____

   _____

Meeting evaluation

1. To what extent are agendas for meetings you attend circulated in advance or at the start?

   Not at all   1   2   3   4   5   Always

2. To what extent are you asked to provide input on the agenda?

   Not at all   1   2   3   4   5   Completely

3. To what extent do participants monitor the way they work together?

   Not at all   1   2   3   4   5   Completely

4. To what extent are differences among participants encouraged and explored?

   Not at all   1   2   3   4   5   Completely

5. When decisions are made, to what extent are the agreed actions made explicit and followed up in writing?

   Not at all   1   2   3   4   5   Completely

6. To what extent do participants seem aware of their use of time?

   Not at all   1   2   3   4   5   Completely

Comments:

_____

_____

_____

_____

_____

_____

Meeting evaluation

Based upon your own feelings and observations, how would you rate this meeting on the following?

1. To what extent were objectives clearly stated?

Completely   Completely
unclear   1 2 3 4 5 6 7 8 9   clear

2. To what extent was the knowledge of participants used?

Not at all   1 2 3 4 5 6 7 8 9   Completely

3. To what extent was decision-making shared by participants?

Dominated   Completely
by one   1 2 3 4 5 6 7 8 9   shared

4. To what extent did people trust and speak freely to one another?

Not open   Completely
at all   1 2 3 4 5 6 7 8 9   open

5. To what extent were all participants actively involved in the meeting?

Not at   To a very
all   1 2 3 4 5 6 7 8 9   great extent

6. To what extent did leadership style contribute to meeting effectiveness?

Not at   To a very
all   1 2 3 4 5 6 7 8 9   great extent

Meeting evaluation

Please rate the extent to which:

	Almost never	Infrequently	Sometimes	Frequently	Almost always
1. Participants had a chance to express opinions	_____	_____	_____	_____	_____
2. People listened to one another	_____	_____	_____	_____	_____
3. Certain members dominated the conversation	_____	_____	_____	_____	_____
4. Some people's ideas were ignored	_____	_____	_____	_____	_____
5. People seemed satisfied with the group's decisions	_____	_____	_____	_____	_____
6. Participants seemed confused	_____	_____	_____	_____	_____
7. People seemed to understand one another	_____	_____	_____	_____	_____
8. People argued with one another	_____	_____	_____	_____	_____
9. People seemed annoyed with one another	_____	_____	_____	_____	_____

Comments

_____

_____

_____

Meeting evaluation

1. Objectives of the
   meeting were: 9   8   7   6   5   4   3   2   1

   Completely   Unclear
   understood   misunderstood

2. Time use was: 9   8   7   6   5   4   3   2   1

   Very   Not
   effective   effective

3. Exchange of
   views was: 9   8   7   6   5   4   3   2   1

   Open and   Not open
   candid   cautious

4. Conflicting points
   of view were: 9   8   7   6   5   4   3   2   1

   Fully   Not
   resolved   resolved

5. Teamwork during
   the meeting was: 9   8   7   6   5   4   3   2   1

   Excellent   Poor

In any situation where performance was not up to the desired
standard, what can be done to improve it? Be specific.

_____

_____

_____

_____

_____

_____

Meeting evaluation

Circle the number that best describes how well our group works together.

	Low							High
Task accomplishment	1	2	3	4	5	6	7	8
Use of time	1	2	3	4	5	6	7	8
Use of people's ideas	1	2	3	4	5	6	7	8
Conflict resolution	1	2	3	4	5	6	7	8
Goal clarity	1	2	3	4	5	6	7	8
Teamwork	1	2	3	4	5	6	7	8
Effective listening	1	2	3	4	5	6	7	8

What can be done to improve our working together?

_____

_____

_____

_____

_____

_____

_____

Practise setting ground rules for meetings
Consider a group that you meet regularly. Think of things that usually happen and classify them as either detracting from, or contributing to, group effectiveness. Then draw up some tentative ground rules around these types of behaviour.

Detracting behaviour	Contributing behaviour

Ground rules to overcome detracting behaviour and reinforce contributing behaviour.

1. _____

2. _____

3. _____

4. _____

5. _____

6. _____

Providing feedback

Feedback allows a person to receive information about his or her effect on others. It can help an individual to keep his or her behaviour 'on target' and better achieve goals. Consider the following illustration. Only through feedback does a person learn the effects that his or her actions have on others.

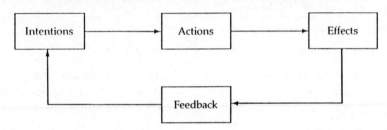

As the leader, it is appropriate for you to provide feedback. Feedback will usually be about an individual's behaviour that either helped the meeting to accomplish its purpose, or was disruptive. It is important to provide positive feedback to participants when they do something that contributes to the meeting's effectiveness.

Criteria for useful feedback

- *Be descriptive rather than evaluative.* By describing action, it leaves the individual free to use or ignore the information. The avoidance of evaluative language reduces the prospect of an individual's reacting defensively.

- *Be specific rather than general.* To be told that one is 'dominating' is not as useful as to be told that not listening to what others said may cause you to miss a valuable idea.

- *Direct feedback about behaviour that the receiver can do something about.* Frustration is only increased when a person is reminded of shortcomings over which he or she has no control.

- *Time it well.* In general, feedback is most useful at the earliest opportunity after the behaviour.

- *Ensure it is communicated clearly.* One way of doing this is to have the receiver rephrase the feedback to see if it corresponds to what the sender had in mind.

Examples of feedback
Learning how to provide helpful, effective feedback is a skill that can be learned. The following examples should give you an understanding of the differences between good and poor feedback.

Poor feedback	Better feedback
1. You are crude and disgusting.	1. Your suggestive stories are embarrassing.
2. You are rude and inconsiderate.	2. You did not allow me to finish. This makes me feel you don't value my comments.
3. You're unfriendly.	3. I feel I'm being left out. Is there some reason for this?
4. You're a loudmouth.	4. Because you talked more than others at the meeting, I didn't get a chance to explain my position.
5. You enjoy putting people down.	5. I feel you didn't seriously listen to my point of view.
6. You don't care about anyone but yourself.	6. You seem unconcerned about others and what they can contribute.
7. You ran the meeting all wrong.	7. I'm frustrated that we were unable to come to a decision. What can we do better next time?
8. You are a wonderful person.	8. I am grateful that you came to my defence.

Check what you learned in Chapter 4

Consider the following statements and mark each true or false based on the material in Chapter 4.

True/false

_____ 1. Motivation to change is not required to improve meetings.

_____ 2. Evaluations can be obtained while a meeting is in progress.

_____ 3. Self-evaluations are usually sufficient to improve meetings.

_____ 4. Trained unbiased observers can be the most effective evaluators.

_____ 5. Evaluation forms are mainly to record participant reactions in order to stimulate problem-solving.

_____ 6. Evaluations after the meeting generally receive more participant attention than those obtained during the meeting.

_____ 7. More than one attempt at improvement may be required before a problem in conducting meetings is cleared up.

_____ 8. Regularly scheduled staff and committee meetings do not need to be evaluated.

_____ 9. Useful feedback is evaluative rather than descriptive.

_____ 10. How to give helpful, effective feedback is a skill that can be learned.

See page 95 for recommended responses.

CHAPTER 5
Summary and Conclusion

A model for effective meetings

You can conduct more effective meetings by practising the ideas presented in this book.

First, decide whether or not a meeting needs to be held at all. Avoid the trap of meeting too often. Be willing to cancel a meeting or adjourn early if there is nothing important to discuss. Deciding whether or not to meet depends on the objective you want to achieve. Once you establish an objective, you may find there is a better way to accomplish it than a meeting.

If a meeting is appropriate, decisions must be made about when and where to meet and who should attend. When choosing a time, keep the needs of participants in mind. Avoid particularly busy times. The meeting site should be comfortable and free from distractions. It should comfortably accommodate the attenders. When choosing participants, be guided by who can either gain from attending or contribute by attending. Keep the number down to the minimum necessary to accomplish your purpose.

Next, develop an agenda and notify participants of the meeting. The agenda should list, in sequential order, items to be dealt with. It should also show the date and time of the meeting plus any scheduled breaks and a targeted ending time. A copy of the agenda should be sent to all participants whenever possible. When it is not possible to distribute an agenda in advance of a meeting, one should be developed as the first item of business.

On the day of the meeting the leader should arrive at the

venue early. During this time, it is important to check the room arrangement and change it if necessary; also, to check audio-visual equipment to ensure that it is operational.

The meeting should begin promptly at the scheduled time. An opening statement should include the meeting's objective, a brief review of the agenda, and any appropriate ground rules, such as 'no smoking'.

In an information meeting, information should be presented in a clear, concise, easily understood style.* Monitor the level of interest as reflected through non-verbal signs. Use voice levels to keep the energy level high. If interest seems to lag, change the format by asking questions. Get the group involved.

In a decision-making meeting, it is essential to facilitate the group's problem-solving/decision-making process. Monitor group interaction and suggest procedures to help make decisions. When there is too little interaction, generate discussion. When there is too much interaction, keep things focused and sum-marise progress. Techniques for displaying and analysing data, generating alternatives, and choosing among alternatives will help to keep the group moving towards the objective.

Regardless of the type of meeting, it is important to close with a restatement of objective, a summary of what was accomplished, and a list of agreed action that needs to be taken.

After the meeting, it is essential to follow up with action. A brief memorandum of conclusions should be written and distrib-uted. Inform appropriate people who did not attend the meeting about essential decisions made.

Finally, each meeting should be viewed as a learning ex-perience. Future meetings should be improved by soliciting evaluations and deciding what action is required to conduct better meetings.

The checklist and action summaries that follow will be helpful reminders of what you need to do to conduct effective meetings in the future.

---

* An excellent book on this subject is *Effective Presentation Skills* by Steve Mandel.

The essential elements of an effective meeting

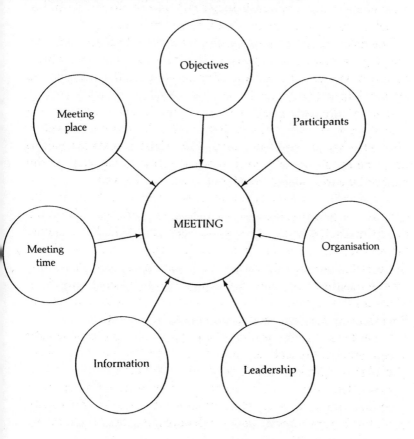

Summary checklist for conducting effective meetings

☐ 1. Clarify the purpose of the meeting.

☐ 2. Select appropriate physical setting and room arrangement.

☐ 3. Use an appropriate leadership style.

☐ 4. Secure group agreement on expectations about agenda, time, objective, and ground rules.

☐ 5. Don't allow the group to jump to conclusions. Suspend judgement and explore alternatives.

☐ 6. Use conflict to differentiate ideas and feelings before attempting to integrate them.

☐ 7. Work for group consensus where knowledge is fragmented and decisions must be supported.

☐ 8. Examine interaction whenever feelings and behaviour do not conform, opinions are not readily offered, or the meeting seems ineffective.

☐ 9. Insist on commitments to action which are specific in terms of what is to be done, follow-up, and responsibility.

☐ 10. Evaluate each meeting with the intention of soliciting a positive plan for improvement for future meetings.

Test your knowledge of effective meetings
Consider the following statements and indicate whether you agree or disagree with each.

Agree/Disagree

_____ 1. A meeting is always the best way to communicate information to a group.

_____ 2. A meeting should be held whenever there is a problem to solve.

_____ 3. A meeting can always be considered effective if you achieve your desired objective.

_____ 4. Most ineffective meetings can be avoided through good planning and preparation.

_____ 5. Effective meetings require the active involvement of all participants.

_____ 6. An important part of preparing for a meeting is to ensure that the right people attend.

_____ 7. Meeting facilities are not important if participants are interested in the subject of the meeting.

_____ 8. Poor scheduling can doom a meeting to failure.

_____ 9. An effective leader should be able to answer all questions asked by participants.

_____ 10. Fear of embarrassment is often the reason for lack of participation.

_____ 11. An effective leader should monitor participation and invite comments from less involved participants.

_____ 12. Questions should be phrased to elicit elaboration on a point.

_____ 13. A good opening statement will help to clarify the meeting's objective.

_____ 14. Meetings should start and end on time.

_____ 15. A good summary will include a restatement of the meeting's objective, a listing of accomplishments, and specific action that needs to be taken.

_____ 16. Participants should leave a meeting feeling that their time was well spent.

_____ 17. Practice helps to produce effective meetings.

_____ 18. The leader always knows how well a meeting went.

_____ 19. Proper meeting evaluation includes input from participants.

_____ 20. A trained observer can contribute to improving a meeting's effectiveness.

_____ 21. Participants can do little to prevent a meeting from becoming ineffective.

_____ 22. Others resent a participant who tactfully contributes to an effective meeting.

_____ 23. A summary should be written and distributed following a meeting.

_____ 24. If an agenda for action is agreed, a confirming memorandum should be sent after the meeting.

_____ 25. Follow-up is often the difference between running a good meeting and achieving results.

See page 95 for recommended responses.

The necessary steps to an effective meeting

Before the meeting

Leader

1. Define objective
2. Select participants
3. Make preliminary contact with participants to confirm availability
4. Book meeting room and arrange for equipment and refreshments
5. Prepare agenda
6. Invite participants and distribute agenda
7. Get in touch with non-participants
8. Make final check of meeting room

Participants

1. Reserve time on schedule
2. Confirm attendance
3. Define your role
4. Determine leader's needs from you
5. Suggest other participants
6. Know the objective
7. Know when and where to meet
8. Do any required preparations

During the meeting

Leader

1. Start promptly
2. Follow the agenda
3. Manage the use of time
4. Limit/control the discussion
5. Elicit participation
6. Help to resolve conflicts
7. Clarify action to be taken
8. Summarise results

Participants

1. Listen and participate
2. Be open-minded/receptive
3. Stay on the agenda and subject
4. Limit or avoid side conversations and distractions
5. Ask questions to ensure understanding
6. Take notes on your action items

After the meeting

Leader

1. Restore room and return equipment
2. Evaluate effectiveness as meeting leader
3. Send out meeting evaluations

4. Distribute memorandum of discussion
5. Take any action you agreed
6. Follow up on action items

Participants

1. Evaluate meeting
2. Review memorandum of discussion
3. Brief others as appropriate
4. Take any action agreed to
5. Follow up on action items

Recommended responses to questionnaires

Check what you learned in Chapter 1, page 15

1. True	6. True
2. True	7. True
3. True	8. True
4. False	9. True
5. False	10. False

Check what you learned in Chapter 2, page 34

1. False	6. False	11. True
2. True	7. True	12. False
3. False	8. False	13. True
4. False	9. True	14. False
5. True	10. True	15. False

Effective use of questions, page 52

1. c	6. e
2. h	7. h
3. f	8. g
4. d	9. a
5. i	10. b

Handling difficult situations, page 57

1. a,c,b,d
2. a.c.b.d
3. a.b.c.d
4. a.b.c.d
5. c.d.b.a

6. a.d.c.b
7. a.d.c.b
8. b.c.a.d
9. d.b.c.a
10. c.b.a.d

Check what you learned in Chapter 3, page 69

1. Content; interaction; structure
2. a
3. Brainstorming to create a solution; nominal group technique to report information already known by the group.
4. False
5. True
6. False
7. d
8. False
9. True
10. True
11. a,c,d
12. True
13. False
14. True
15. Understand what is expected, be on time, participate, don't be disruptive, support the leader, listen, be objective, carry out agreed action.

Check what you learned in Chapter 4, page 86

1. False
2. True
3. False
4. True
5. True

6. True
7. True
8. False
9. False
10. True

Test your knowledge of effective meetings, page 90

1. Disagree
2. Disagree
3. Disagree
4. Agree
5. Agree
6. Agree
7. Disagree

8. Agree
9. Disagree
10. Agree
11. Agree
12. Agree
13. Agree
14. Agree

15. Agree
16. Agree
17. Disagree
18. Disagree
19. Agree
20. Agree
21. Disagree

22. Disagree
23. Agree
24. Agree
25. Agree

Further Reading from Kogan Page

The Company Secretary's Handbook, Helen Ashton
How to Make Meetings Work, Malcolm Peel
How to Take Minutes of Meetings, Jennie Hawthorne
Never Take No For An Answer, Samfrits Le Poole